BUILDIN… …NCE

Bill Redmon, PhD

with Ian Redmon, MFA

Introduction

Resilience is one of the most widely used but misunderstood concepts in our popular jargon. From education to sport to community capacity following a natural disaster, people talk "resilience." The capacity to "re-build" after a hurricane, play well after throwing an interception, or get good grades despite a history of child abuse have all been called resilience. Two main fallacies permeate this common use and understanding of resilience; first, that some person, organization, or community "is" resilient and second, that resilience is a trait – you have it or you don't – and if you have it you keep it. But those are misperceptions. Resilience is a capacity that grows – in a person, organization, or community; resilience does not simply "pop up"—it develops. And it develops and is strengthened under specific conditions. Ironically, stress is what creates resilience.

Physiological systems, individuals, and organizations become more flexible, stronger, and capable when challenged by moderate, predictable, and controllable stress. In contrast, extreme, prolonged, and uncontrollable stress tears down physiological systems, individuals, and organizations. The capacity to face a stressor, respond in an appropriate fashion, and return to baseline functioning present prior to the challenge is a manifestation of resilience. Yet by facing that challenge, part of the resilience "reserve" is consumed. And even the most resilient wear down without opportunities to rest, replenish, and re-set. Resilience, then, ebbs and flows as a function of the nature and pattern of our stressors.

This book is an introduction to some of the concepts related to the intentional creation of individual and organizational practices and conditions that will improve the capacity to demonstrate resilience in the face of significant challenges. These concepts seem simple, yet the result of implementation can be remarkably powerful. Individuals and organizations are dynamic, complex systems; an awareness of how to grow and strengthen our capacity to demonstrate resilience is transformative. Stress, distress, and catastrophic events in life and work are inevitable, but when the reserves of resilience are high, these experiences need not result in disease, dysfunction, and despair. This book can help teach us more about building those reserves of resilience.

Bruce D. Perry, MD, PhD

Meet Tree 76, a redwood in California's Muir Woods.

TREE 76

Redwoods are capable of thriving for thousands of years. They are resistant to pests and the hottest fires.

As it ages, a redwood's defenses strengthen, layer by layer. In fact, the older it gets, the faster it grows.

Tree 76 is just 785 years old. Even the average specimen is an icon of resilience.

The resilience and longevity of redwoods is no accident. Over millenia, the species has evolved to match the unique dangers of its environment. Its grooved bark—which can be up to twelve inches thick—gives it insulation from wildfires.

Redwoods also contain high levels of tannin, which gives them their signature color. When other tree species are damaged by fire, they quickly become infected with fungi and are likely to die. However, if a fire manages to penetrate a redwood's bark, tannin is released to the damaged area, protecting the tree from infection.

You have more in common with these majestic trees than you might think. Humans don't produce a comparable "tannin." But by learning more about our own brains and changing our habits and thinking patterns, we can grow as we age, building reserves of resilience to draw from in times of uncertainty.

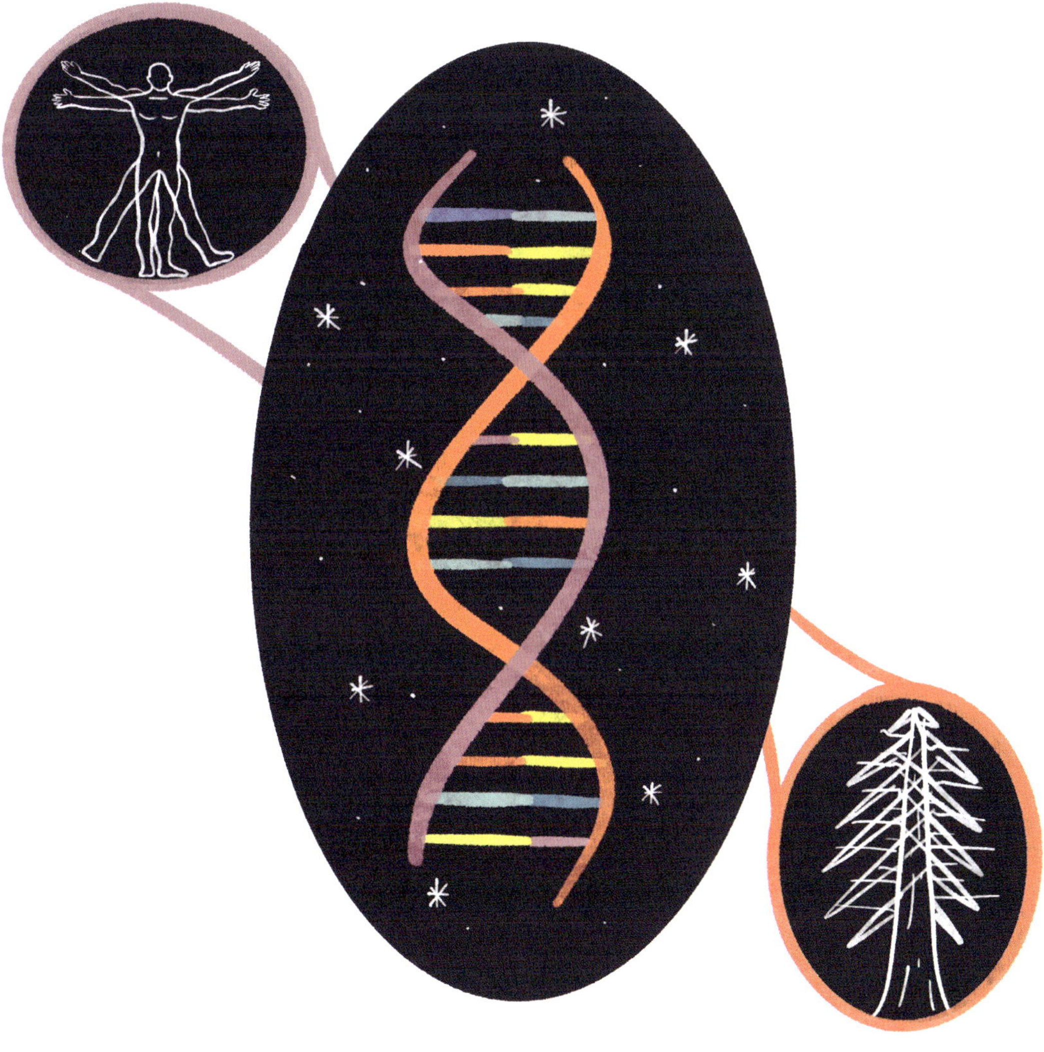

In a human context, resilience is the ability to bounce back from difficulties and adjust to change. People who cultivate resilience don't try to stop negative emotions altogether, nor do they know how to solve every problem they face—a tight deadline at work, or a conflict with a family member, for example. Instead, they develop strategies that allow them to avoid overwhelm and manage everyday stressors with confidence.

When life gets tough, people with resilience move through their stress and keep going.

We all have different life experiences and levels of stress sensitivity. And some people have less power over the stressors in their life than others do. Still, each of us has something to gain when we tune into our emotions. Resilience is a muscle anyone can strengthen over time.

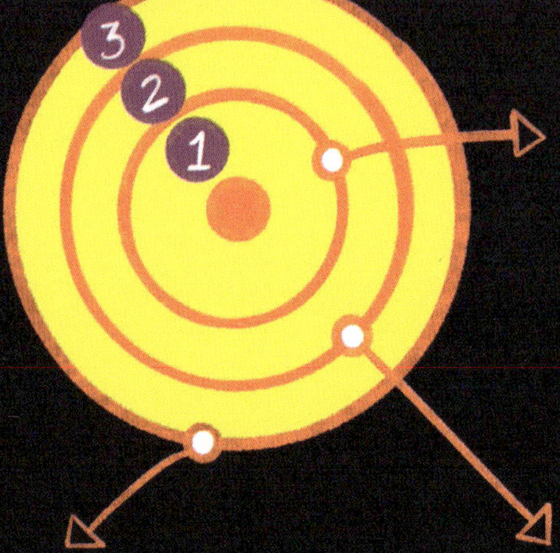

YOUR #1 emotional ZONES

#2 REGULATION FOR RESILIENCE

YOUR DAILY #3 OPERATING RHYTHM

Across three chapters, this book will introduce you to three ideas grounded in neuroscience.

Chapter 1: Your Emotional Zones

"Our thoughts, feelings, and actions are influenced by the structure of the human brain."

Chapter 2: Regulation for Resilience

"Practicing emotional regulation strategies during times of stress is key to building resilience."

Chapter 3: Your Daily Operating Rhythm

"Creating a daily operating rhythm is a powerful way to sustain reserves of resilience."

YOUR

#1 emotional

zones

What's in a name?

Awareness of your emotions and the impact they have on you is a powerful skill and a building block for resilience. It's hard to believe at first, but the simple act of naming what you're feeling and why you're feeling it will give you more control over stress and enable you to affect yourself and the people around you in positive ways.

In one study, people upset about delivering a speech became calmer after they labeled their anxiety.

92% of supervisors with strong emotional awareness have teams with high energy & high performance

emotions and influence

Emotional awareness is important in influencing others. In the workplace, supervisors who can identify their own emotions can better manage how they affect others, especially if they can preempt negative reactions and become more supportive and helpful.

It is clear that emotional self-awareness is critical to building resilience and influencing others. Unfortunately, most of us are not very good at identifying what we are feeling or what to do about it. But that can improve.

HOW the BRAIN HANDLES STRESS

The path to resilience requires that we learn to notice and manage changes in our emotional states and our brain's response to them. As our response to stress changes, the part of our brain that is active changes. The thinking brain engages when we are calm. The emotional and primitive brains activate when we are frustrated, alarmed, or afraid.

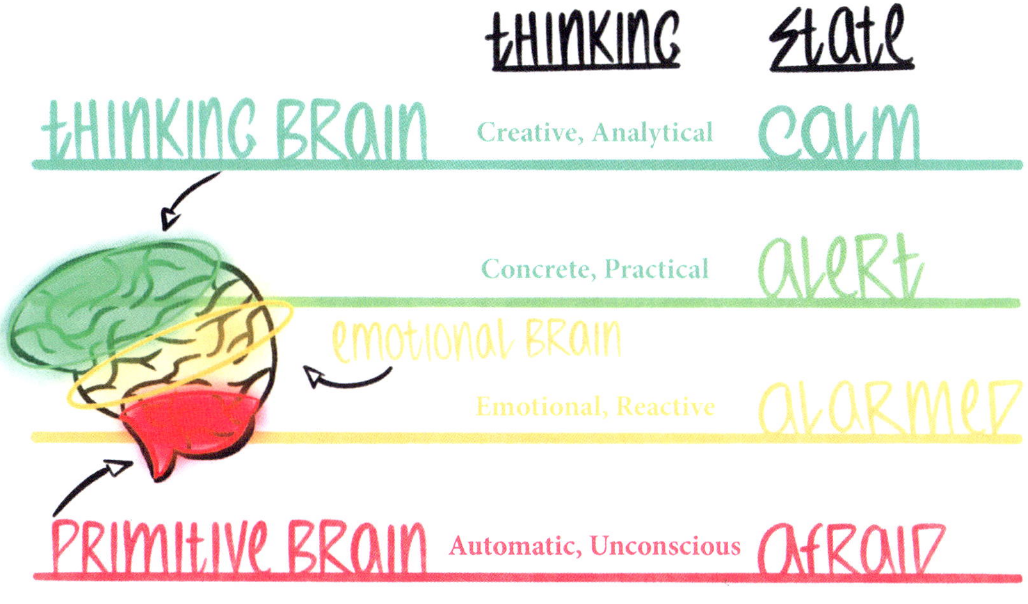
Thinking
State
Thinking Brain
Creative, Analytical
Calm
Concrete, Practical
Alert
Emotional Brain
Emotional, Reactive
Alarmed
Primitive Brain
Automatic, Unconscious
Afraid

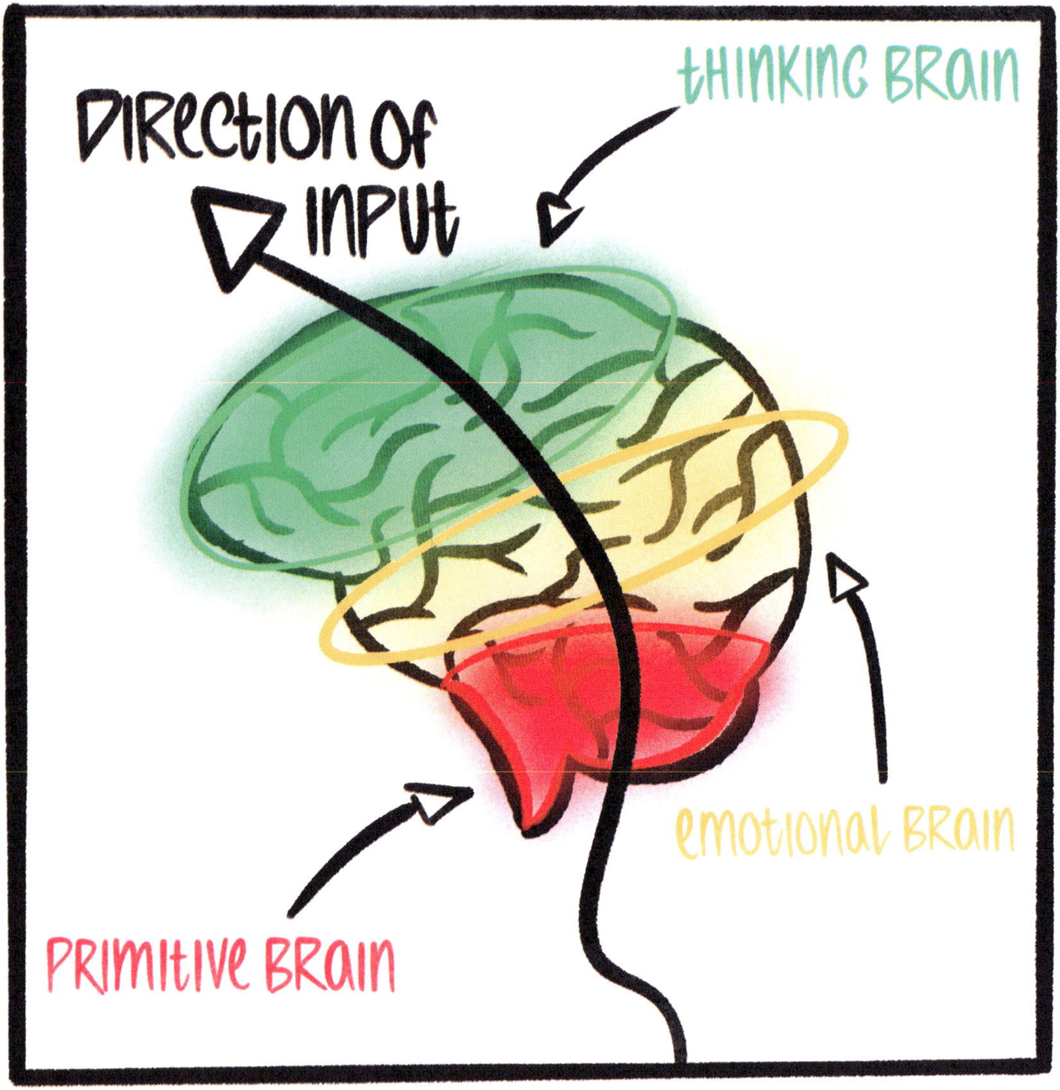

Direction of input
thinking brain
emotional brain
primitive brain

Decoding the Ancient Brain

All information from inside and outside our bodies travels through the brain from the bottom up, which means that the more primitive part of the brain always has the chance to respond first. If incoming information looks like a threat, the primitive brain reacts before information can flow to other parts of the brain for more complex processing.

The primitive brain is built for speed. For example, if a car is barreling towards you, your primitive brain takes over and helps you react quickly to get out of the way.

Unfortunately, this same primitive brain may react strongly to things that don't require it. Our brains have evolved much more slowly than our civilization has progressed, and they aren't sufficiently equipped to assess the 'threats' we encounter on a daily basis. You may get physically upset over an email or text with a critical tone, or a low performance rating, or even a frown from someone important. These situations don't require the same response as a car barreling towards you, but the brain activates as if they do. The primitive brain is doing exactly what it's supposed to, yet this default response can limit your thinking power when you need it the most.

VS.
Re: MISSED DEADLINE

THINKING

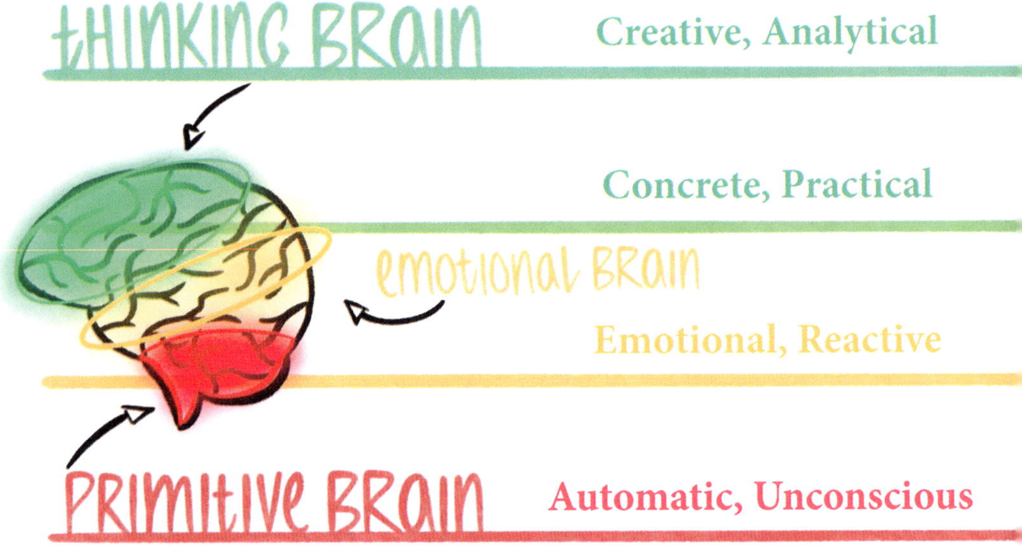

© Dr. Bruce D. Perry/Kintla

The brain's response to stress directly impacts our emotional state and the part of the brain that is active. As emotions and brain states change, it affects working IQ. When we are calm, our IQ is high. When we are alarmed or afraid, our IQ drops.

State	Functional I.Q.	Zone
calm	100-120	Green Zone
alert	80-110	Green Zone
alarmed	60-90	Red Zone
afraid	50-70	Red Zone

When we are calm and focused, information flows past the primitive brain to the thinking brain where we can process it effectively. People who keep their thinking brain engaged under pressure build resilience over time.

When we are guided by our thinking brain, we are at our best—solving problems creatively, feeling good about our performance, and treating others with care and respect. This is the Green Zone. When we are operating in our primitive brain we enter a cycle of reactivity. Our instinct to fight, flee, or freeze can be triggered by the smallest criticism from a spouse or a coworker. What's more—our fear is so distracting that we are more likely to make mistakes, produce sloppy work, or stall entirely. This is the Red Zone. At times, we can become unfocused, distracted, fatigued, and disengaged. In this case, our automatic brain takes over and we operate based on habit, with little thinking involved. In this state, we may cross the street while checking our phone, drive to work without remembering the trip, or send an email full of errors. This is the Gray Zone.

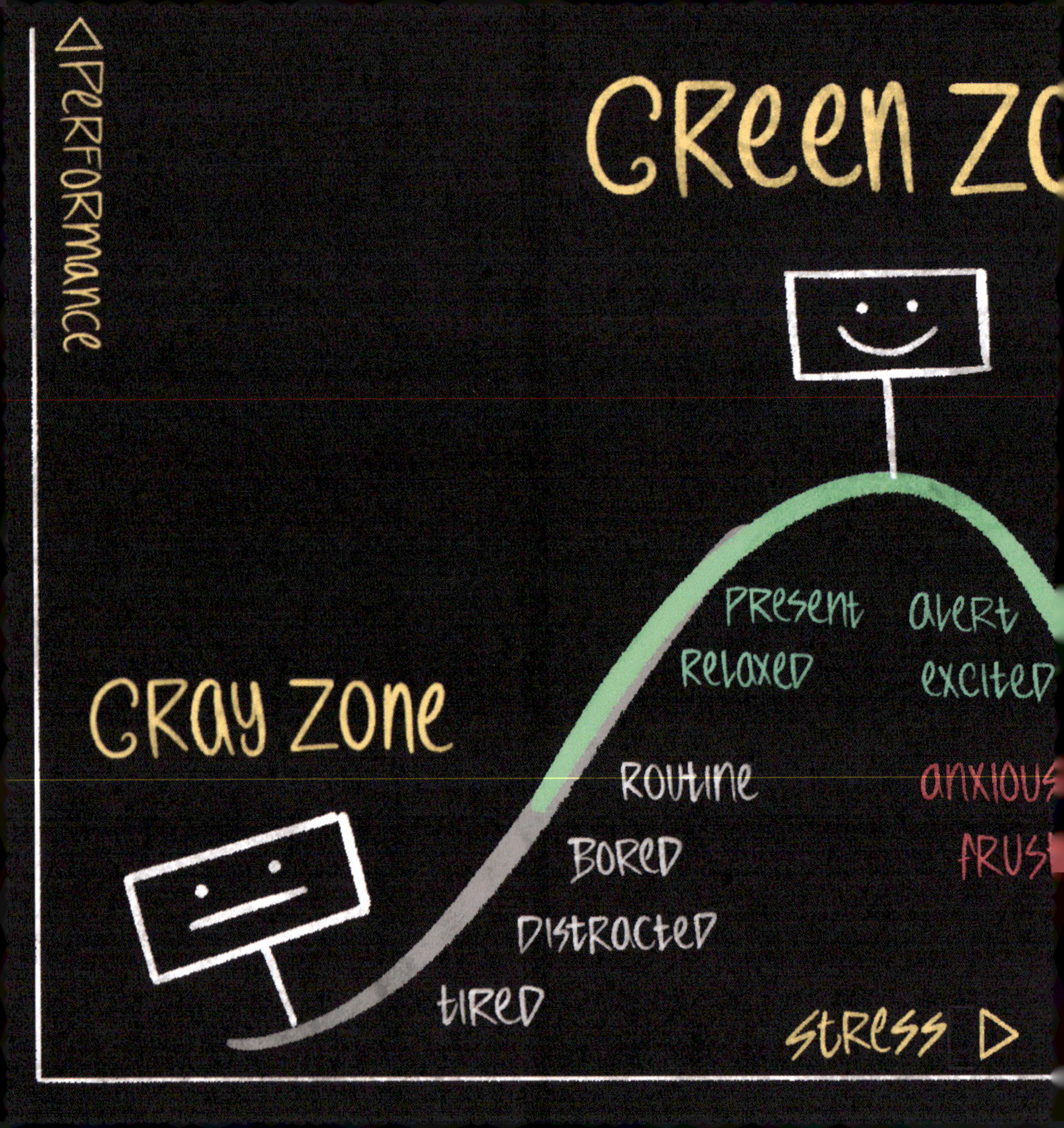
PERFORMANCE
Green Zo
Gray Zone
present
alert
relaxed
excited
routine
anxious
bored
frus
distracted
tired
stress

This curve shows that some stress is necessary to keep us engaged and performing well. Every minute of every day, our effectiveness in life changes based on how we handle stress. When stress is high and we can't manage it, we enter the Red Zone where reactivity is high and our operating IQ and performance are low. When stress is low and we don't reset our attention, we enter the Gray Zone where we tend to lose focus and become less effective.

We can increase resilience by noticing when we are rotating into the Red or Gray Zones and managing stress to move back to Green where we are interested and performing at our best.

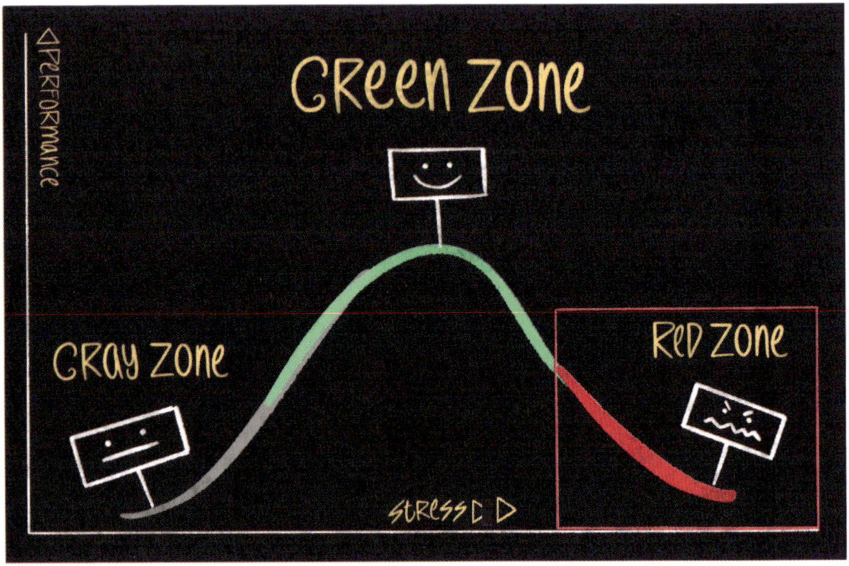

Let's explore the Red Zone, as this is where people often end up under pressure. On the edge of the red we may feel tense or nervous, but as the stress continues, we advance to alarm and a full-blown Red Zone event. This level of stress makes it difficult to think and work until we calm down.

Remember that Red Zone responses are not always very active like anger or arguments. Sometimes, people simply go quiet, but they are not calm under the surface.

RED ZONE TRIGGERS

"When people don't do what they say they'll do."

"When I have to repeat myself multiple times."

"When my boss sends me a request at six in the morning."

Let's take a closer look at the Gray Zone, which is where our emotions take us when stress is low and our habitual, automatic brain takes over. Rather than assessing the environment for threats, the brainstem relies almost exclusively on what it has experienced before to make decisions. Depending on the situation, the effect of time spent in the Gray Zone can be dangerous. Imagine you're working on a complex electrical task at a construction site. Even a few minutes in the Gray Zone could prove deadly.

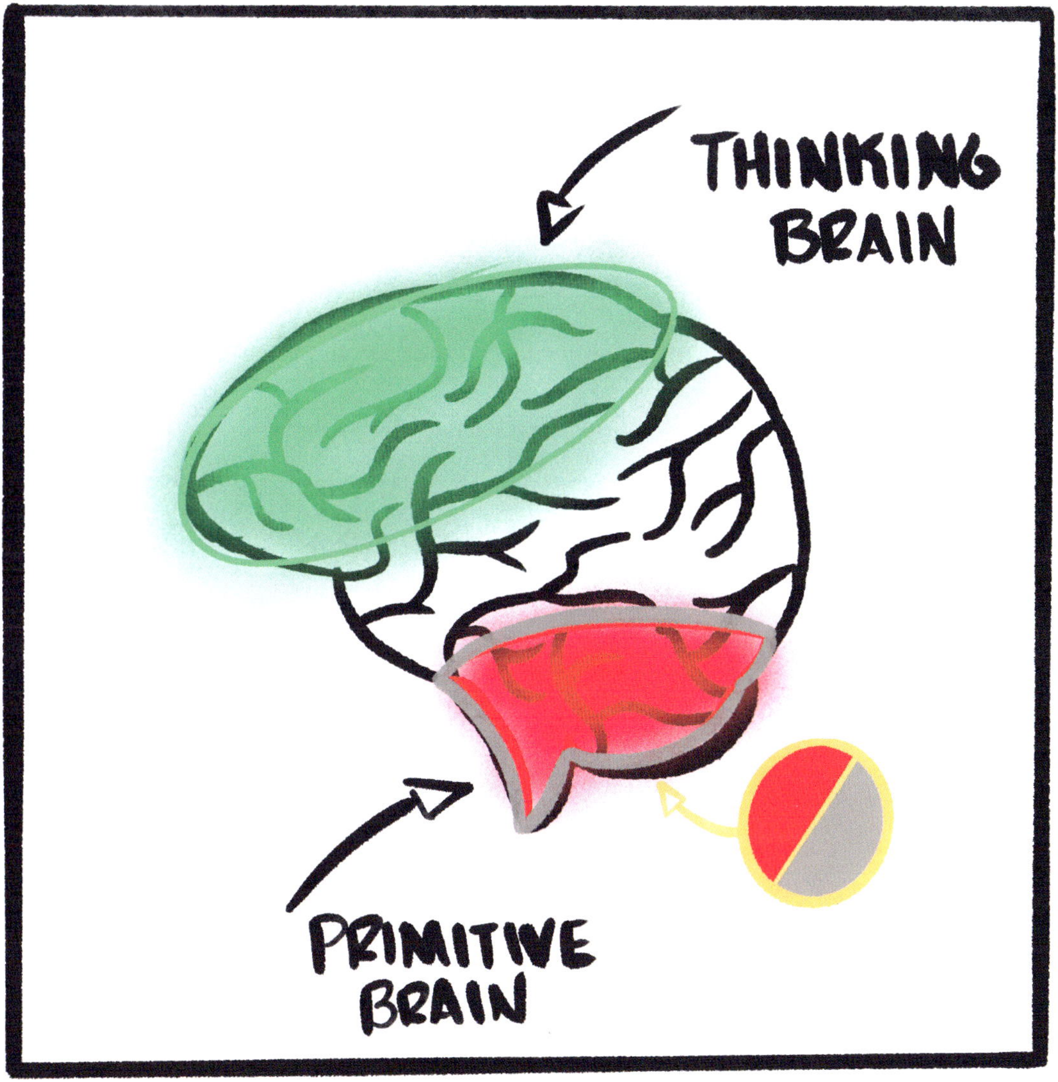
THINKING BRAIN
PRIMITIVE BRAIN

The diagram on the next page shows how the effects of Gray Zone thinking become more pronounced the longer we're in the Gray Zone. For this reason, it's essential that we notice as soon as we enter the Gray Zone and take action to refocus our attention.

LOWS BECOME
LOWER AND LONGER

Resilience requires that we manage our emotions to reduce the impact of stress. Because we can't rely on our brains to keep us calm or focused as stress levels change, we have to notice what is happening and override the system by practicing emotional regulation strategies. In the next chapter, we'll discuss a range of options designed to help you build sustainable resilience.

Regulation

#2

for

Resilience

It's not magic - It's habit

It's easy to think of resilience as a magical skill that appears for some people when a project or task becomes overwhelming. When stress levels rise, people with reserves of resilience are able to remain calm, manage setbacks, and find a way to move forward. But these reserves don't appear out of thin air—resilience develops through the practice of regulating emotions and acting in an effective way under pressure. Learning these techniques while you're in the Green Zone will help you more easily recall and use them when you face significant stress. With enough dedication and practice, anyone can learn how to employ these tools and build reserves of resilience over time.

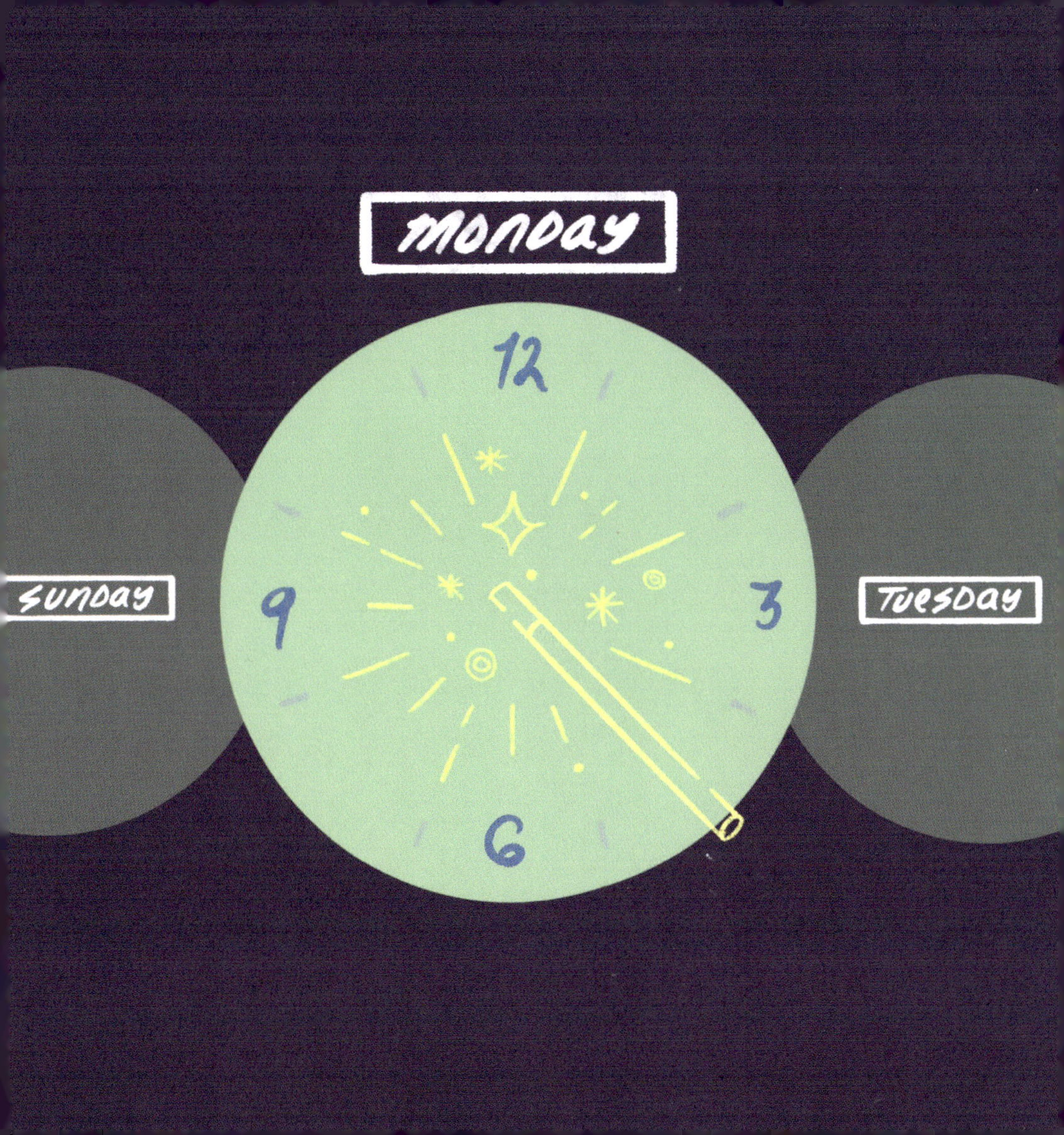
MONDAY
SUNDAY
TUESDAY
12
9
3
6

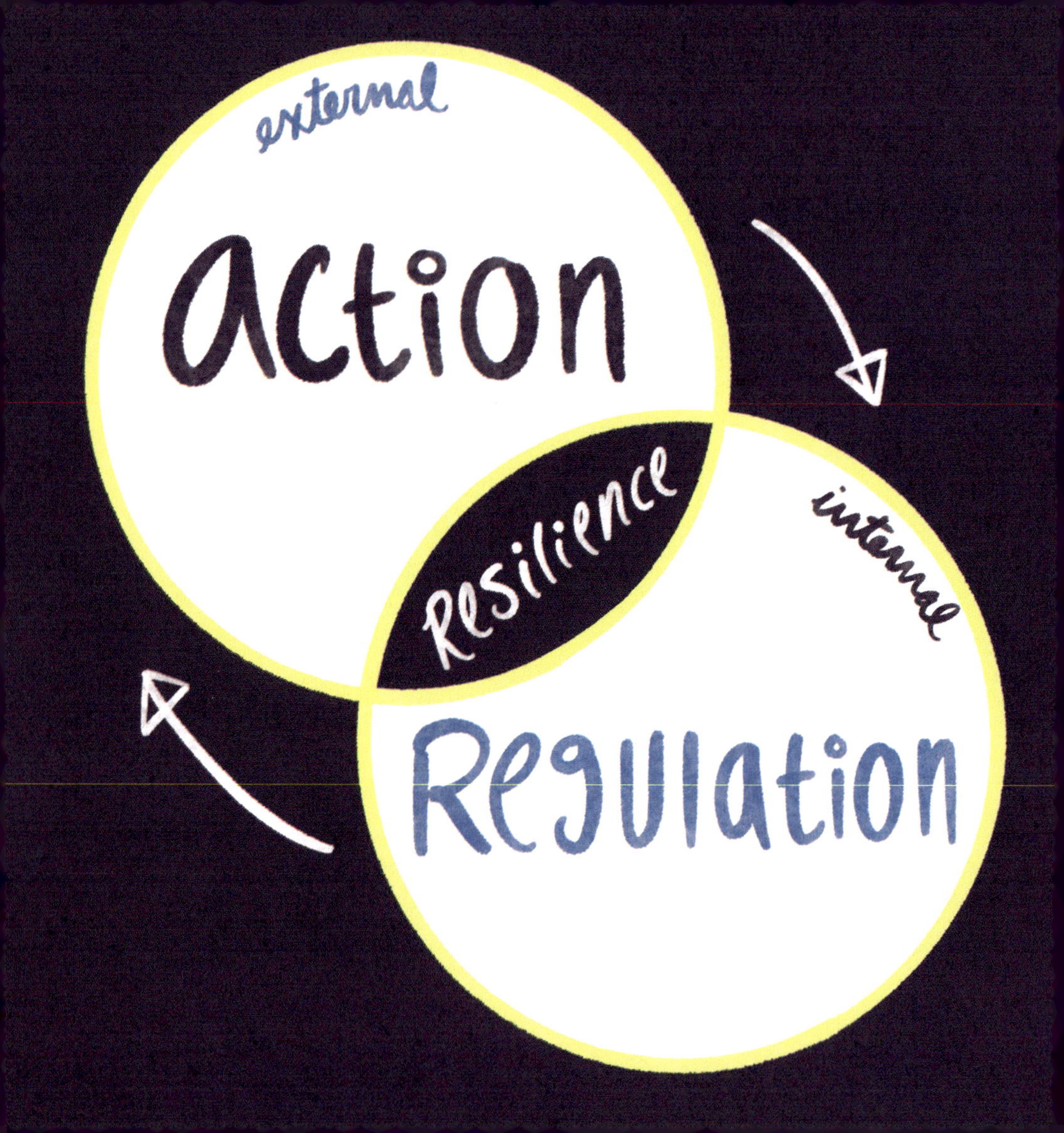
external
action
Resilience
internal
Regulation

We’ve already talked about emotional states as zones. When people practice resilience, it means they are able to influence the zone they are in, even under stressful conditions.

Two strategies are key to sustaining a state of resilience: external action—that is, what we do in response to stressful events or in stressful situations—and regulation, which refers to the intentional strategies we use to influence our minds and our bodies.

The strategies available to us to regulate our bodies and our emotions can be divided into three categories—Top-Down, Bottom-Up, and Relational. A successful regulation regime includes strategies from all three categories.

TOP-DOWN
Strategies that focus on shifting your thinking as a means of making stressors seem less stressful.
RELATIONAL
Interactions with others who support you and can help you regulate through processing stressful events or by distracting you in a positive way.
BOTTOM-UP
Strategies that focus on influencing your physiology as a means of reducing the physical and mental effects of stress.

Bottom-Up Regulation

Sample Techniques

Relax your muscles.

Breathe deeply—in through nose, out through mouth.

Go somewhere warmer or colder.

Take a walk.

Look at nature.

Try it

Muscle Relaxation

Repeat the steps below for each of the pictured muscle groups.

1. Breathe in and tense your muscles for 10 seconds

2. Breathe out, and suddenly and completely relax your muscles

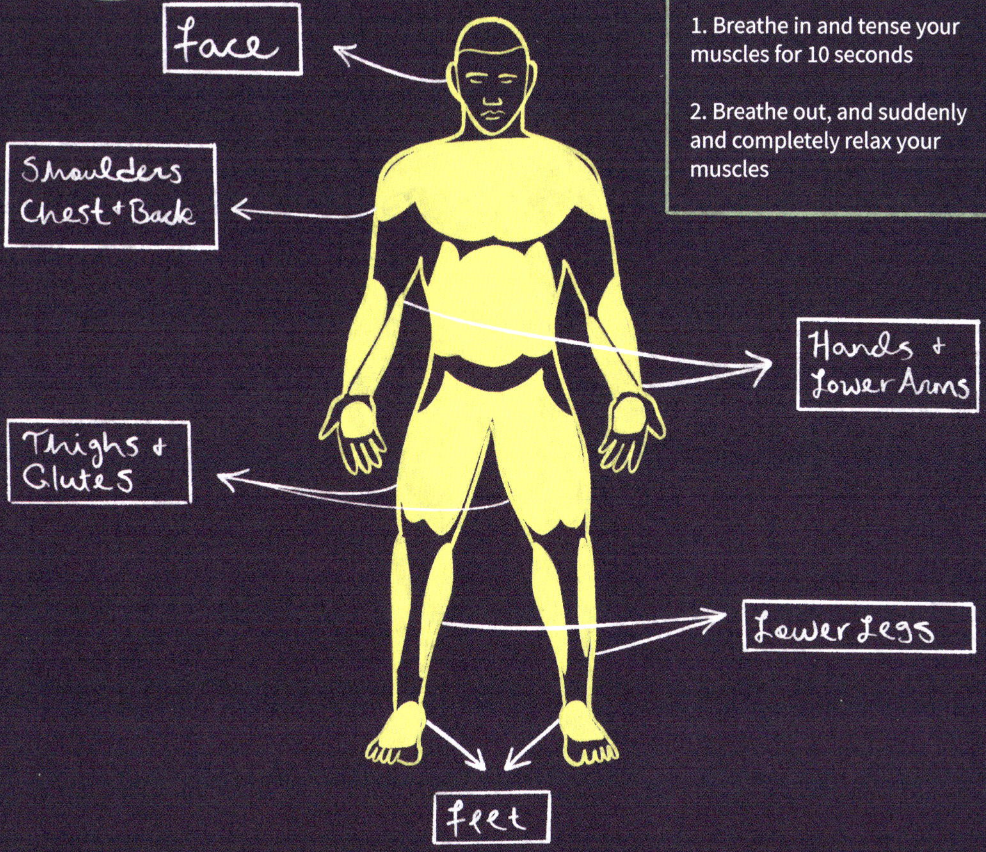

FieldNote

"Sometimes, I get trapped by my negative thinking and focus on what is wrong and how bad it is. When this happens, I try to zoom out to make the stress small. I go from close up to wide angle to satellite and change my relationship with the stressor. For example, I say, what will I think of this day when I am 95?"

Top-Down Regulation

Sample Techniques

Practice positive self-talk.

Focus on goals.

Identify elements of your situation you can control.

Reframe.

Label what you're feeling.

Try it

Reframing

1 **Notice**

Notice the emotion you are feeling.

2 **Name**

Name the emotion and any thoughts connected to the emotion.

3 **Reframe**

Identify a positive, competing thought that challenges or changes the way you feel.

FieldNote

"Sometimes, when people bring me another problem, I get upset about their lack of initiative and it stresses them. I have to remember to help them reframe things to see the positive. Our team has done a lot and we've been successful. So, we can handle any problems that come to us. When I remind them that we are good at what we do, it kicks up the energy and gets them attacking the problem."

Relational Regulation

Sample Techniques

Ask others for advice.

Talk about your stress.

Have a quick, positive conversation.

Call a friend.

Show gratitude to another person.

Try it

Positive Conversations

A quick, positive conversation with another person has the potential to help both parties regulate their emotions.

One way to start a quick, positive conversation is by asking someone questions about their perspective on a problem you're facing.

What would you do if you were me?

Have you been in this situation before?

perspective-taking

Remember...

Be brief, and be positive.

You don't need a lot of time to connect with others in a powerful way.

The interactions we have with other people on a daily basis can have a big impact on our resilience. In fact, research tracking social patterns showed that those who had a larger number of positive interactions per day with family, friends, and other peers were more likely to demonstrate resilience under pressure.

MORE RESILIENT
OTHERS
FRIENDS + COWORKERS
Family
1 interaction

Less Resilient
Others
Friends + Coworkers
Family
1 interaction

FieldNote

"Sometimes I get others out of the Red Zone just by asking how I can help. When I see somebody stressing out, I try to keep myself calm and ask them what is happening and how I can help. Sometimes people want help, but mostly they have it covered and just want to be heard."

The Bigger Picture

The regulation techniques we just reviewed can be used throughout our days to stay in the Green Zone. But we can also build a lifestyle that is inherently regulating. One way to do this is to practice regular "gratituding." Thinking about what we appreciate in our lives reduces our stress even if we don't tell anyone about these thoughts. Communicating this gratitude to others publicly is even better. Gratituding can be as simple as making a list of what we are thankful for or actually sending notes or telling people around us what we appreciate about them. Some families use gratituding boards where they post notes that describe what they are thankful for.

Try it

GRATITUDE

Practicing gratitude can take many different forms. A mix of public and private activities makes for an effective routine.

Public Gratitude

Say thank you to someone in person.

Send thank you notes.

Commit an act of kindness.

Compliment others.

Disagree respectfully.

Private Gratitude

Write down three good things at the end of each day.

Keep a daily journal of your positive experiences.

Write down what you do well at home or at work.

#3 YOUR DAILY OPERATING RHYTHM

it's a Given

The things we do every day come to define us—unfortunately, the behaviors that make up our Daily Operating Rhythm are often locked in and difficult to change. The good news is that small changes to our routine can make a big difference.

D.O.R.

DOR: Getting Started

The process of changing your routine begins with understanding what it is now, planning the changes you want to make, and incorporating those changes slowly over time to ensure that change sticks. Think of it as a three step process—Map It, Change It, Lock It In.

The first step is to map your Daily Operating Rhythm by listing your key activities in the order you do them every day, or almost every day.

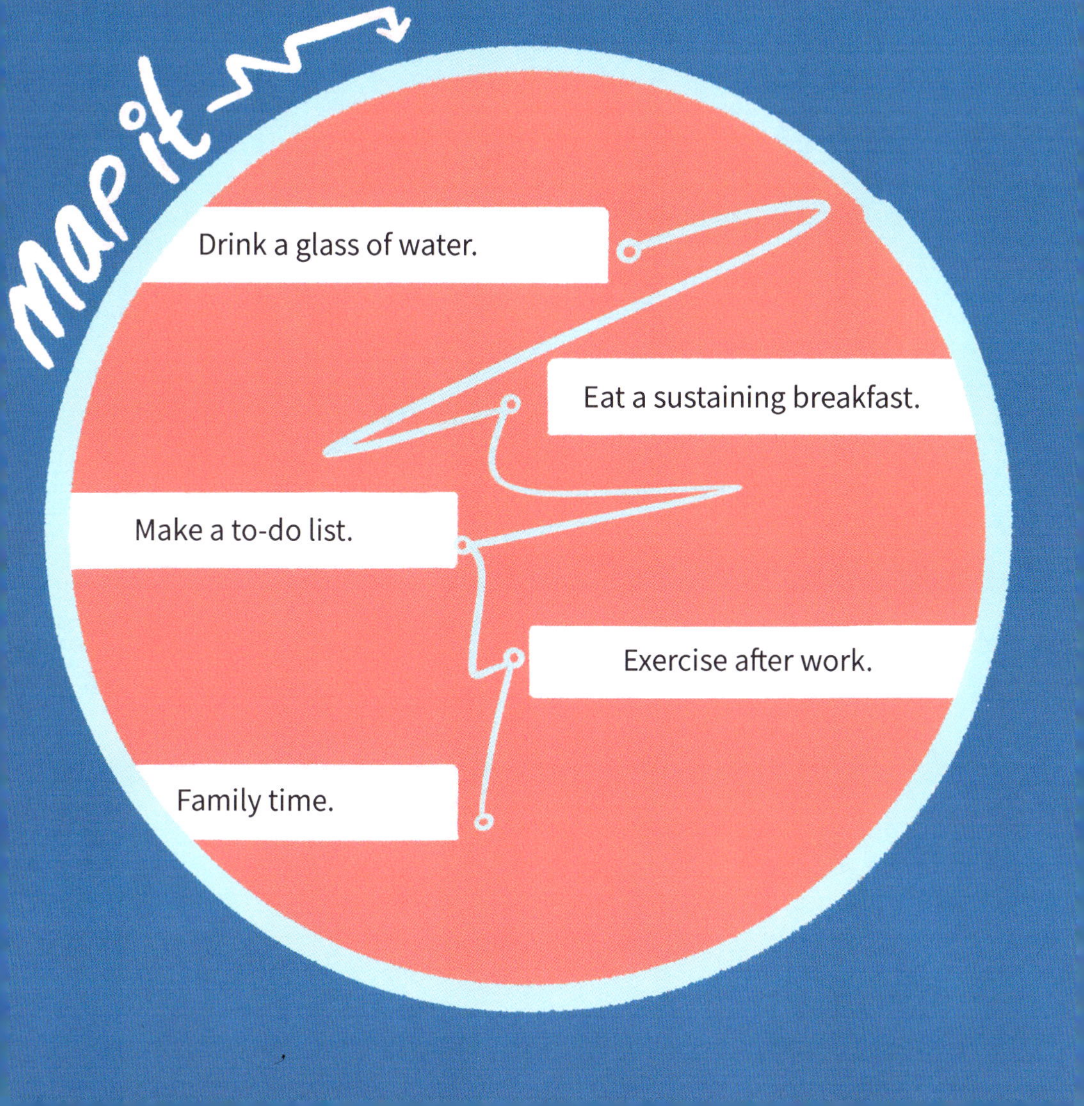
Map it
Drink a glass of water.
Eat a sustaining breakfast.
Make a to-do list.
Exercise after work.
Family time.

MAKING INROADS

When it comes to changing your routine, it isn't always easy to know where to start. One way is to choose key times during the day where there's an opportunity for new habits to make a difference. Once you've chosen a timeframe, it should be easier to decide what new habit might fit there.

Change it

10:00
11:00

Read for 20 minutes before bed.

4:00
5:00

Make a to-do list for the next day before leaving work.

6:00
7:00

Make time to cook dinner (no takeout) five days a week.

The science shows that practicing a new behavior 21 days in a row is an effective way to make it a habit. Once you've chosen a few small habits to pursue, pick the one that's most important to you. Do it every day for 21 days, and you'll find that it's much easier to carry on doing it without much thought or exertion. After 21 days, continue practicing the first habit but add another one—rinse and repeat. Over time, you'll build up an arsenal of habits powerful enough to change your life.

lock it in

Cycle one

Exercise 30 minutes a day, starting February 1st.

Cycle Two

Read for 20 minutes before bed, starting March 1st.

An effective DOR requires constant attention as we refine our ability to regulate emotions and stay resilient. In previous chapters, we established that there is a thinking self and an emotional self, and we reviewed ways to influence our emotions by using regulation strategies including shifting our thinking. To do this, we need to make changes, but also evaluate how they are working and make adjustments along the way. This requires the ability to reflect on what is happening in our thinking and environment.

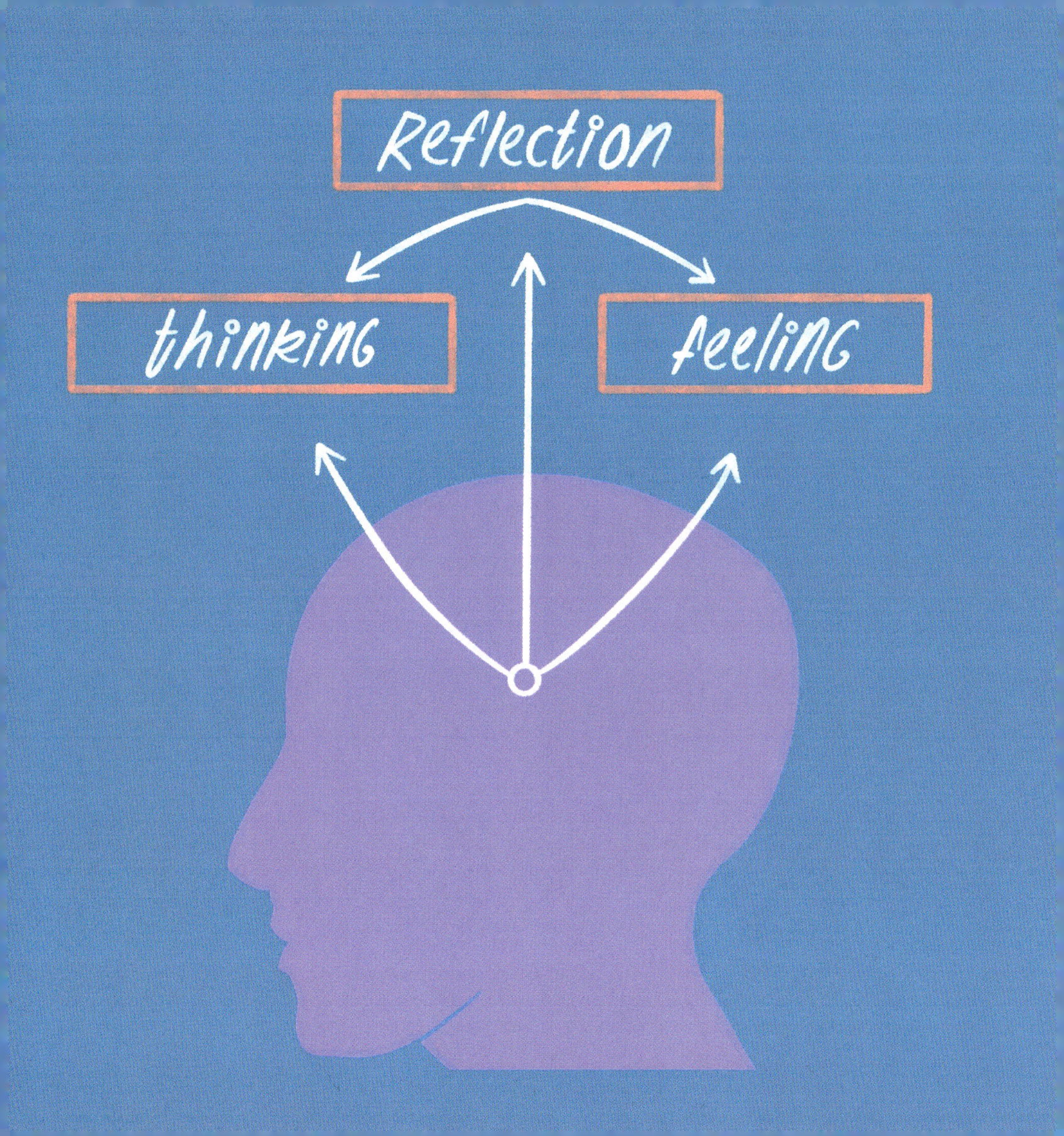
Reflection
thinking
feeling

Reflection allows us to examine our thoughts, our feelings, and the actions we've taken in response to them, as well as how those actions serve us and others. Reflection also leads us to evaluate our basic assumptions in a realistic way. Both of these steps are essential to the DOR sequence—Map It, Change It, and Lock It In.

Try it

Reflection

What did you observe as you tried to make changes in your DOR and form new habits?

How did you feel as you moved through the Map It, Change It, Lock It In process?

Have you been successful in changing habits in the past? What worked, and what didn't work?

How do the changes you are making align with your values? Will this make it difficult to change?

How would you describe your ideal Daily Operating Rhythm? Will the habits you've chosen get you there?

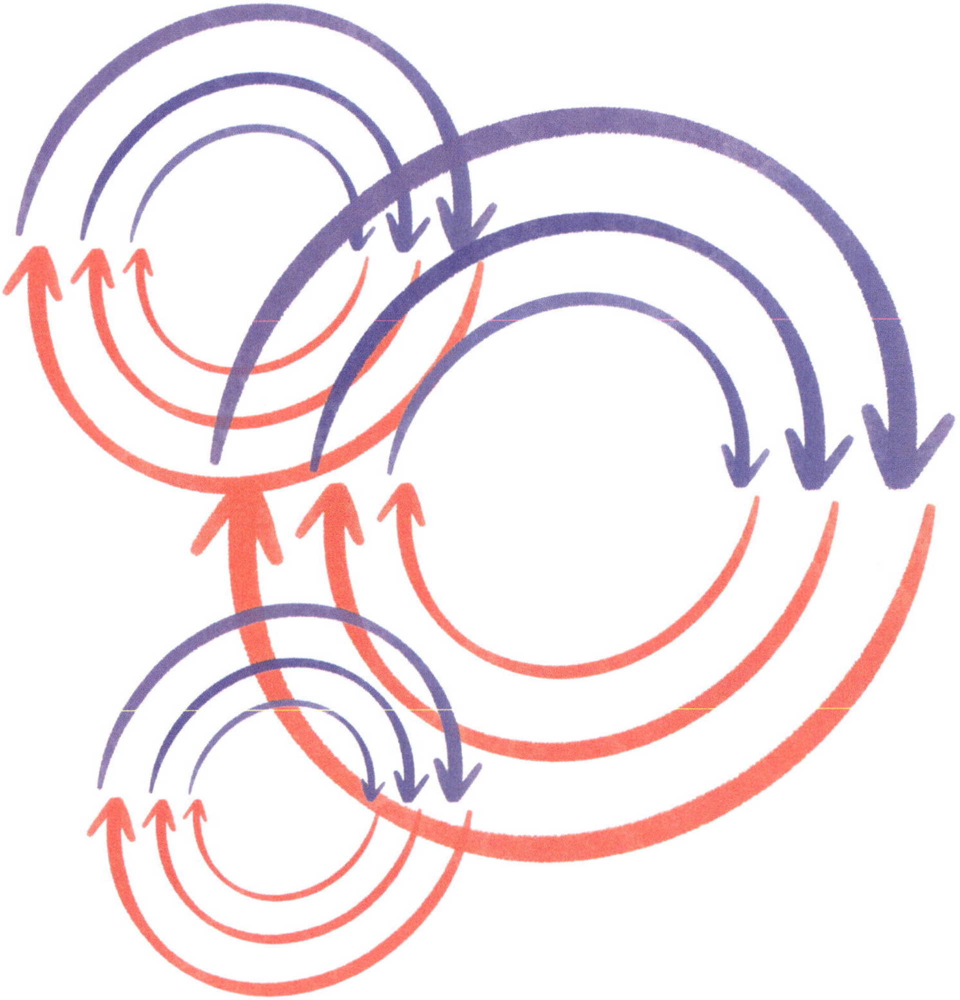

Throughout history, great thinkers, writers, and leaders have managed their Daily Operating Rhythms to achieve their goals, understanding that even the simplest routine allows creativity and productivity to flourish.

Barack Obama

As you can see, there's nothing extraordinary about the former president's schedule.

With routine, it isn't all about the components. What's important about Obama's routine is that he could wake up in the morning and not have to waste time deliberating about what he was going to do and when.

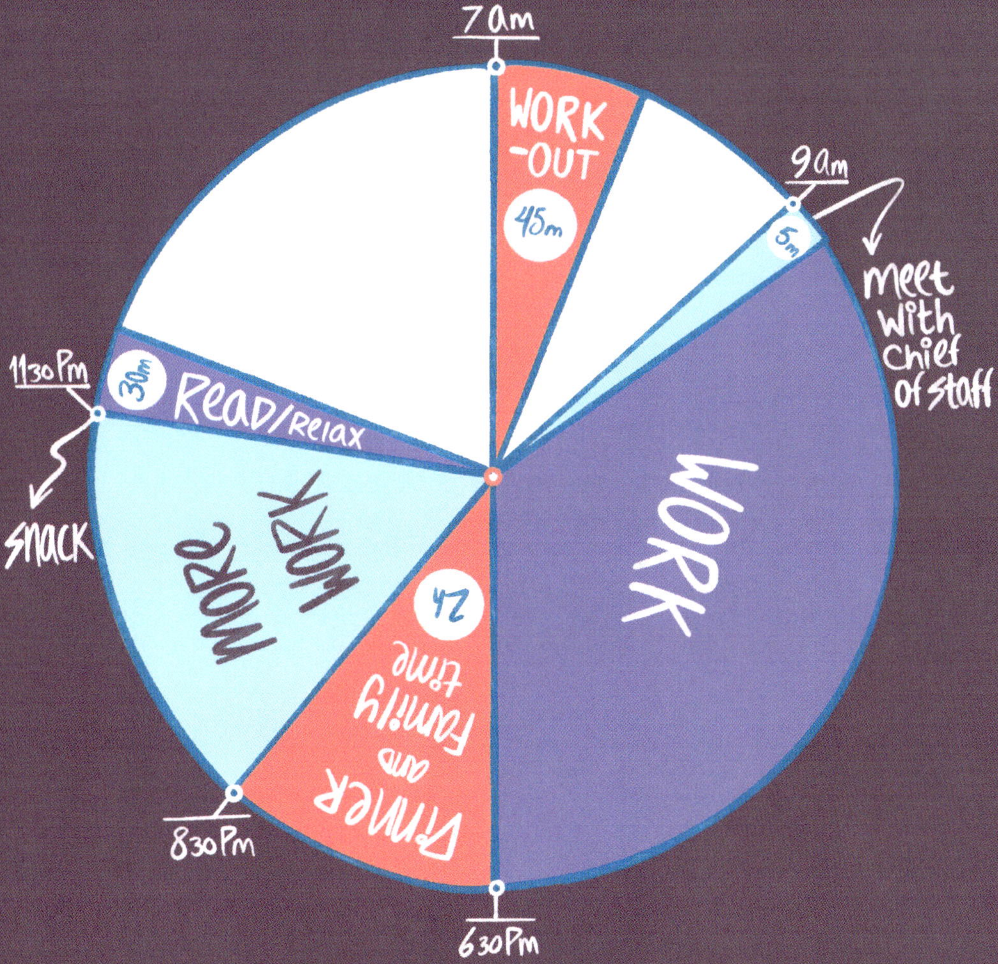

7am
WORK-OUT
45m
9am
5m
meet with Chief of Staff
WORK
630Pm
Dinner and Family time
2h
830Pm
MORE WORK
1130Pm
snack
30m
Read/Relax

Arianna Huffington

After collapsing from burnout and exhaustion thirteen years ago, Huffington prioritizes rest and self-care in her daily routine. Adding self-care activities done at particular times each day allows for deep relaxation and recovery with little impact on the amount of time available for doing work. Thirty minutes of reading is more regulating than three hours of scrolling through social media feeds.

7am → WAKE UP

20m → MEDITATION

40m → EXERCISE

9am → START WORK

7pm → FAMILY TIME

930pm → HOT BATH

10pm → SHUT OFF ALL DEVICES

1 hr → READING AND GRATITUDE

Dolly Parton

No matter how busy her schedule is, Dolly Parton can count on the hours between 3 and 7 a.m. to be free from distraction. Structuring your free time makes it easier to go with the flow during the times of day where you have less control over your schedule. This way, last minute meetings and urgent tasks won't get in the way of the deep work that's essential to long-term growth.

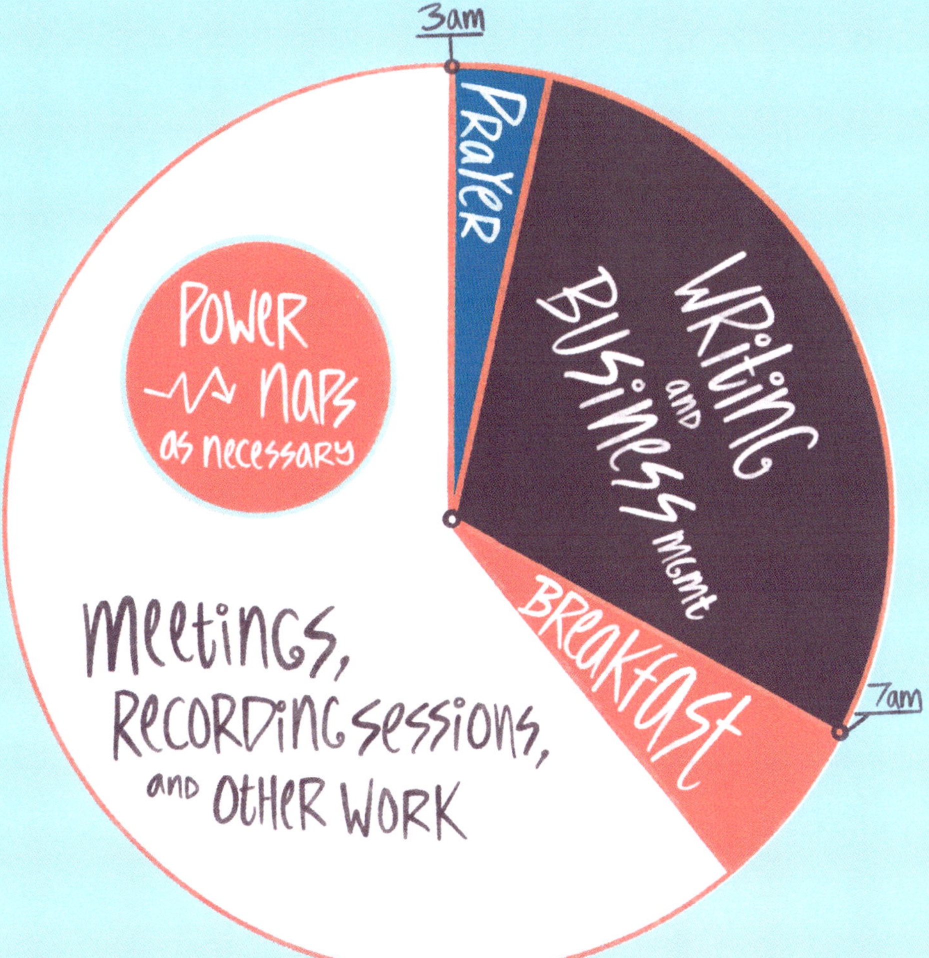
3am
Prayer
Writing and Business mgmt
Breakfast
7am
Power naps as necessary
Meetings, Recording sessions, and other work

Remember, your Daily Operating Rhythm need not require the will of a super hero to be highly effective. It could be as simple as the example below:

7am → Wake up

8am → Make to-do list

11am → Eat protein

1pm → Breathe deeply

30m → Respond to emails

7pm → Take a walk

10pm → Journal

20m → Read

Recap

Let’s review everything
we’ve talked about so far.

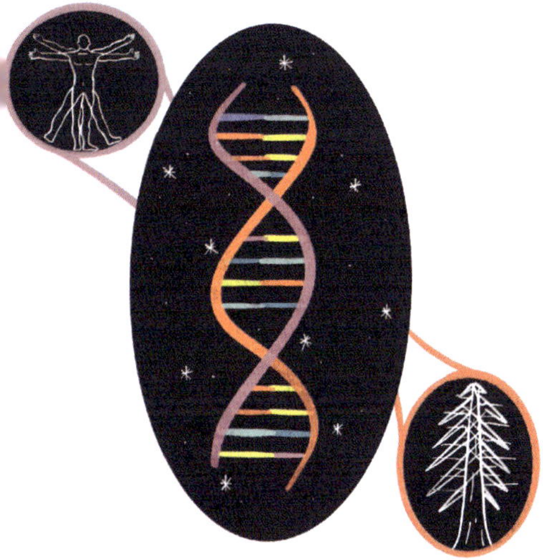

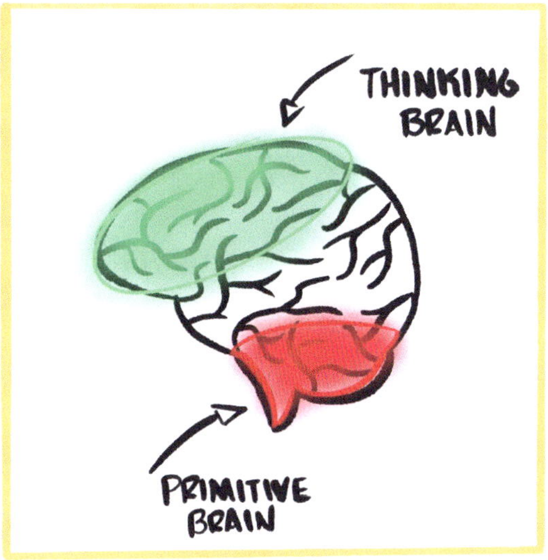
THINKING
BRAIN
PRIMITIVE
BRAIN

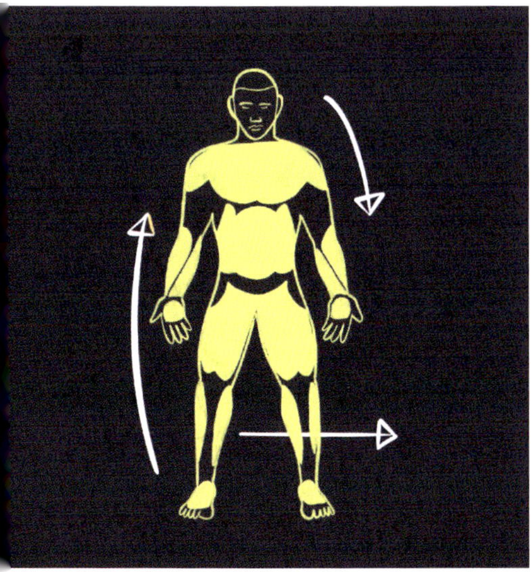

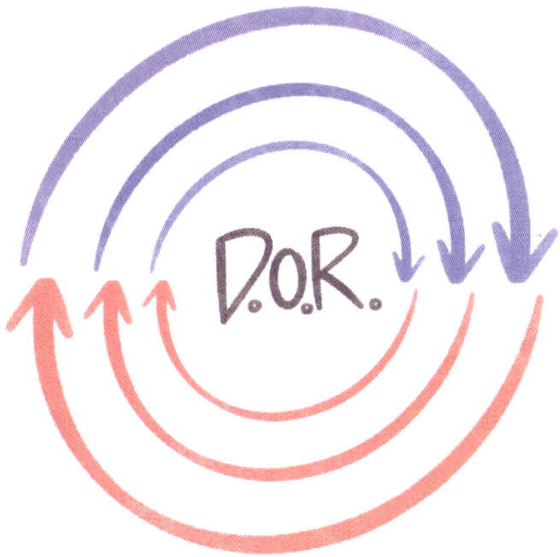
D.O.R.

Unlike the redwood tree, humans don't produce a chemical to protect us from our contemporary environment. However, we can cultivate resilience by adding new practices to our daily routine. Like rings of wood growing around a tree, each practice adds to our reserves as we grow.

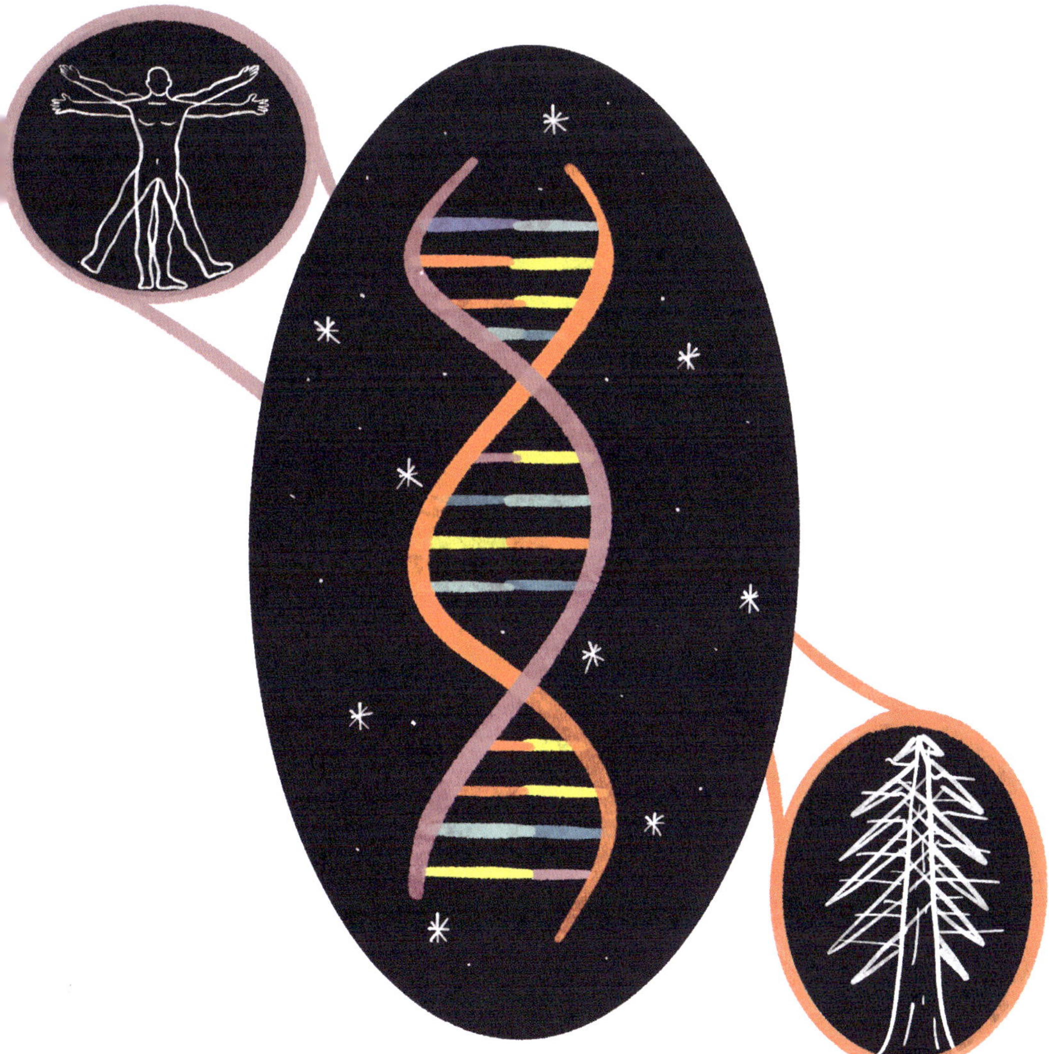

Understanding the evolution of the human brain is key to knowing and influencing our emotions. In turn, emotional awareness and influence on a moment-to-moment basis unlocks sustained happiness and productivity.

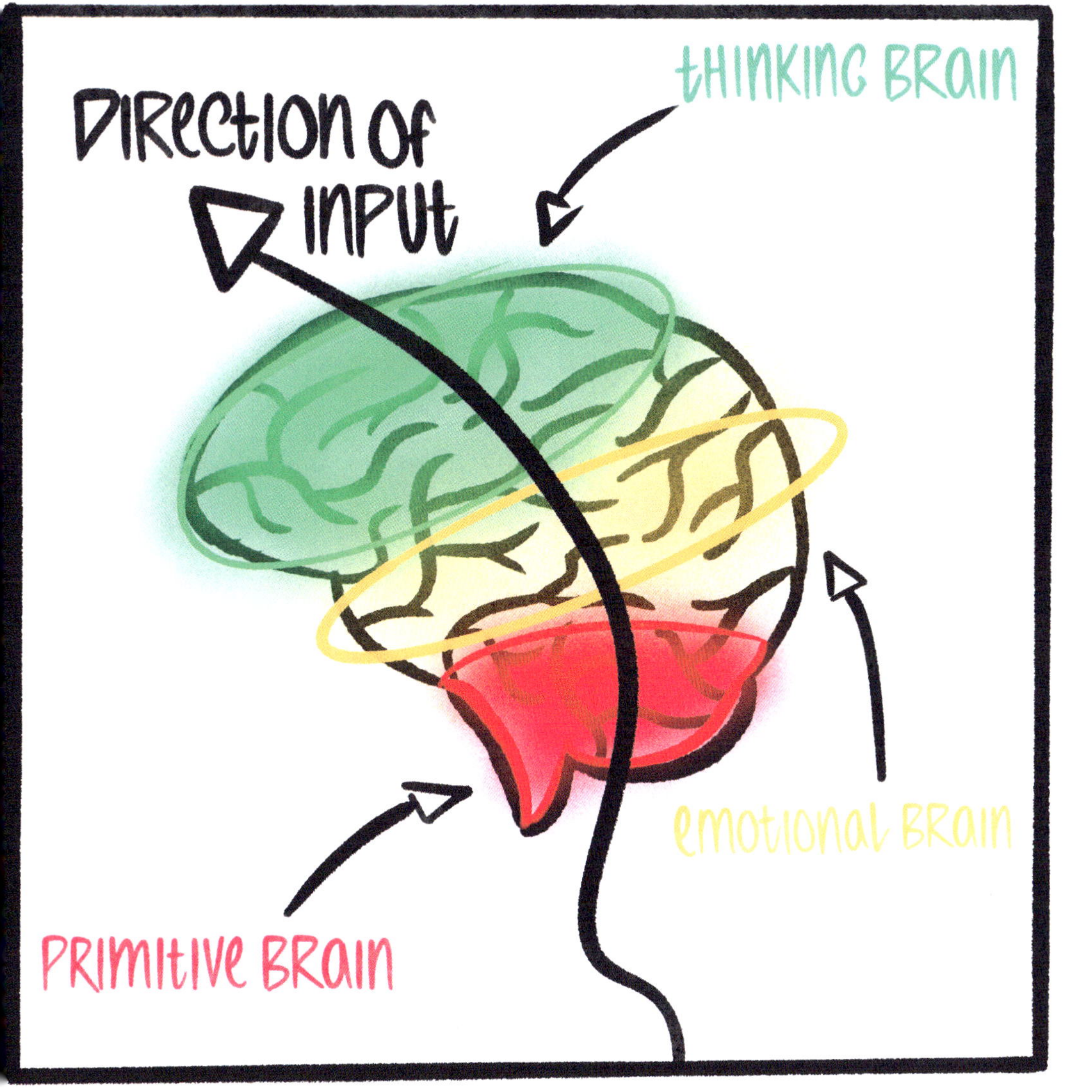
Direction of input
thinking brain
emotional brain
primitive brain

Strategies that influence the stress state of the mind and the body, and thus our emotions, fall into three main categories—top-down, bottom-up, and relational. Using a combination of these techniques, we can change the way we feel in any given moment *and* build resilience over time.

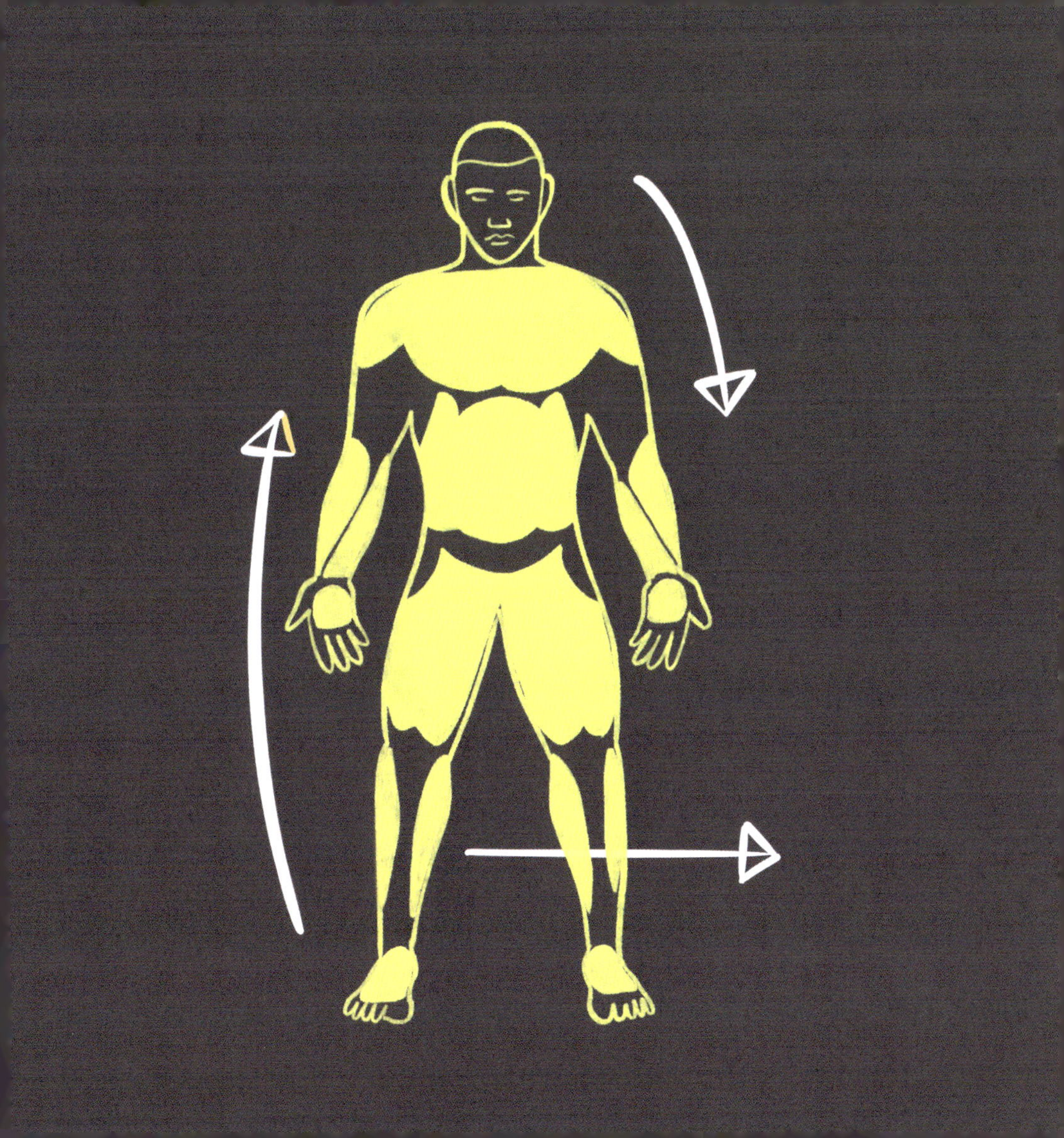

Our Daily Operating Rhythm consists of the behaviors we repeat each day. Integrating regulation strategies into one's Daily Operating Rhythm is an effective way to ensure that emotional awareness and regulation becomes second nature—in other words, resilience is habitual.

D.O.R.

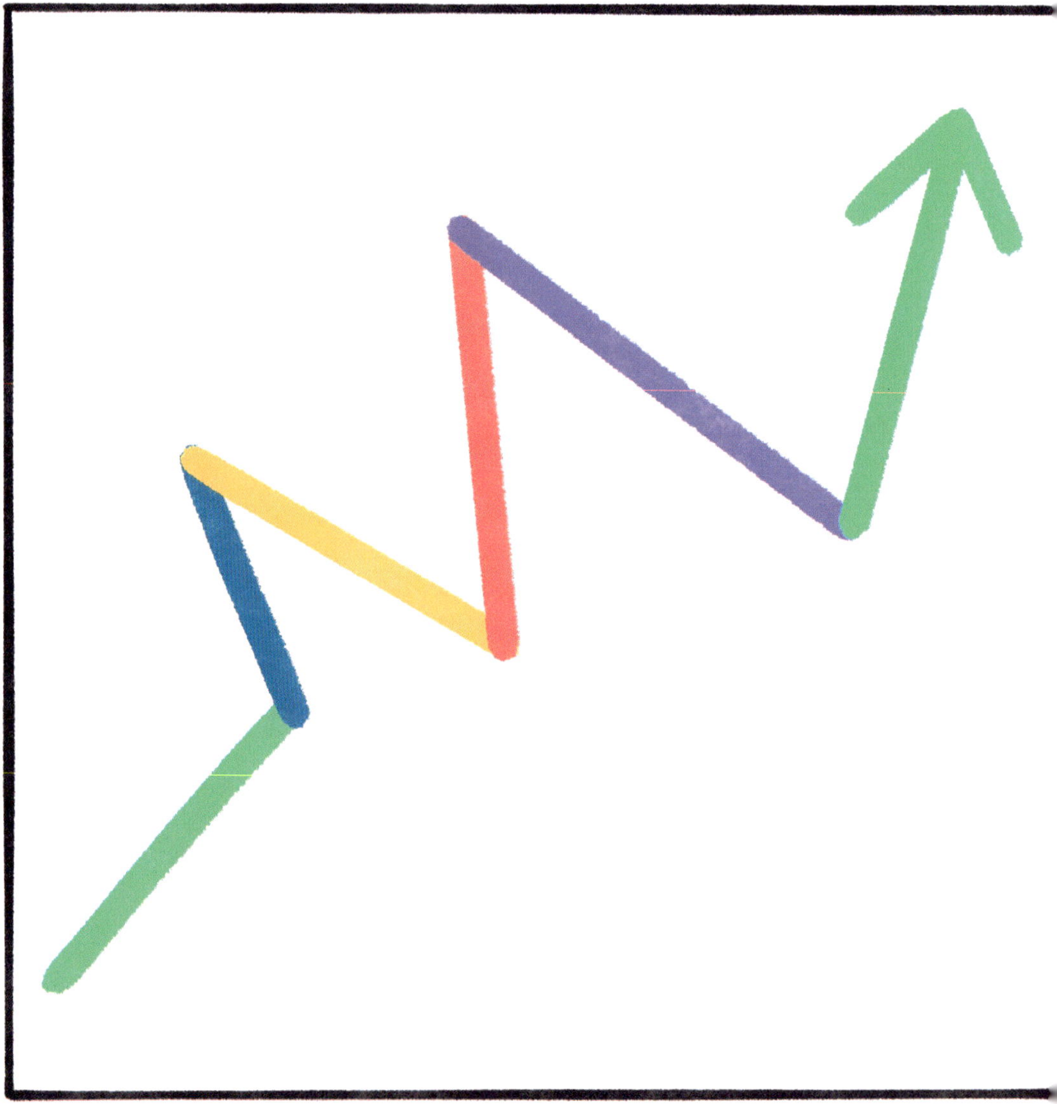

Developing a practice around these new techniques takes time. In the beginning, you may find yourself devoting significant energy to emotional regulation. Keep going. In time, it will become second nature.

And remember, it's not about what you feel—what matters is how you respond to your feelings.

Emotional regulation doesn't require a lack of negative emotions. Even if you execute these steps perfectly, you will undoubtedly have bad days and times of stress, worry, and anger. This is normal. As you face the challenges that come along with creating change in your life, remember—a resilience practice is one of the greatest gifts you can give yourself.

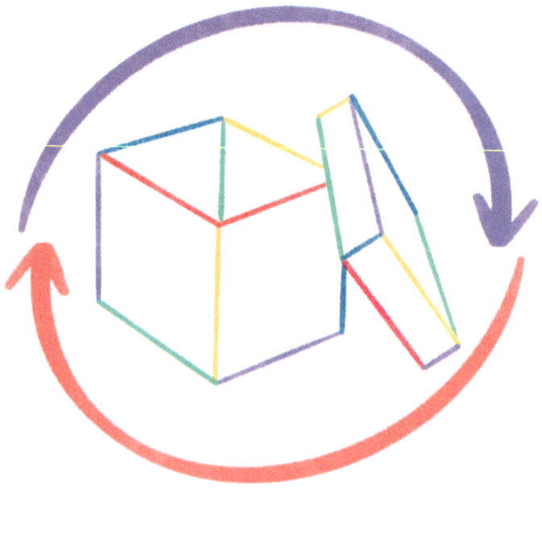

Appendix

of Regulation Strategies

Bottom-Up

- Practice controlled breathing (take several deep breaths and let them out slowly)
- Relax muscle tension (notice and relax major muscle groups starting with the neck and shoulders and working your way down through the back, arms, legs, and feet)
- Take a quick walk (5 min) and notice what is around you
- Stand and disengage from work (turn around and scan the world around you for 1 minute)
- Count to 10, 25, 50, etc. in your head
- Use deep pressure input—squeeze your muscles, push fingers into muscles to focus attention
- Put your head down on the table for a short time
- Take a walk alone
- Look at pictures on your phone or in your work area especially pictures that are soothing (e.g., your children,

pets, locations that are relaxing)

- Look at nature (trees, water, flowers, grass) which research shows is more soothing than manufactured objects
- Smile more—the muscle movements can trigger positive emotions
- Visualize positive experiences—things that made you feel good (visual imagery)

Top-Down

- Redefine stress in a positive way (e.g., I can do this)
- Anticipate “red zones” by looking ahead and getting ready
- Review your values and what you stand for—remind yourself of your higher purpose
- Notice and reduce negative self-talk
- Gratituding: Think of all the things you are grateful for from family and friends

- Identify distorted thinking that causes you anxiety (e.g., you have to be right all the time, obsessing about mistakes)
- When you hit a roadblock or barrier to success, shift perspective to generate options
- Label your emotions: Think about what you are feeling and give it a label such as “frustrated” or “sad” or “angry”
- When you make a mistake, think about what you are going to do to overcome it vs. avoiding it or distracting yourself
- Take responsibility for what is happening versus blaming others which may lead to anger and frustration
- Notice and interrupt negative cycling in thought patterns that become locked in
- Adopt a growth mindset (I can grow, change, adapt) versus a fixed mindset (I am who I am, and it can’t be changed)

Relational

- Talk to others who are supportive and helpful
- Demonstrate empathy and support for others
- Use active listening (eye contact, questioning, etc.)
- Ask others for input/opinions/solutions
- Do something to help other people (it comes back to you)
- Ask others to help you re-think stress when you are stuck
- Communicate with friends/family via text or social networks
- Do something social (go out after work, eat lunch with team)
- Avoid isolation (working virtually) and plan time with others
- Build in time for family and friends and organize it yourself; don't just wait for others to do it (be proactive)

Acknowledgement

The ideas and toolkit presented in this book are based heavily on the pioneering work of Dr. Bruce D. Perry. Over the last thirty years, Dr. Perry has been an active teacher, clinician, and researcher in children's mental health and the neurosciences holding a variety of academic positions. His work on the impact of abuse, neglect, and trauma on the developing brain has impacted clinical practice, programs, and policy across the world.

Dr. Perry's most recent book, *What Happened to You? Conversations on Trauma, Resilience, and Healing* (2021), co-authored with Oprah Winfrey, is a #1 New York Times Bestseller.

Printed in Great Britain
by Amazon

35681405R00064